D1391676

Start Writing
Adventure Stories

Penny King
Ruth Thomson

Belitha Press

First published in the UK in 2000 by

Belitha Press Ltd
London House, Great Eastern Wharf,
Parkgate Road, London SW11 4NQ

Copyright © Belitha Press Ltd 2000
Text copyright © Penny King & Ruth Thomson 2000
Illustrations © Belitha Press 2000

All rights reserved. No part of this book may be reproduced
or utilized in any form or by any means, electronic or mechanical,
including photocopying, recording or by any information storage
and retrieval system, except by a reviewer, who may quote brief
passages in a review.

ISBN 1 84138 207 8 (hardback)
ISBN 1 84138 214 0 (paperback)

British Library in Publication Data for this book
is available from the British Library.

Series editors: Mary-Jane Wilkins, Stephanie Turnbull
Designers: Rachel Hamdi, Angie Allison, Holly Mann
Illustrators: Brenda Haw, Jan McCafferty, Gwyneth Williamson
Educational consultants: Pie Corbett, Poet and Consultant
   to the National Literacy Strategy; Sarah Mullen, Literacy Consultant

Printed in Hong Kong

Contents

WRITING STORIES

Have you ever wondered
how to start a story
or what to write next?
This book will help you.

There are six big pictures like this.
Each picture gives you lots of ideas
for a story. All the words on the
picture are <u>nouns</u> (names of things)
and you can use them to check
your spelling.

Each big picture is followed by
a story plan. The plan is divided
into parts to help you write exciting
stories with a beginning, a middle
and an end. The story plan also
helps you to decide what kind of
story to write.

The story begins

First think about where the story
takes place and decide what might
have happened so far. You need
an exciting opening sentence.

Desert Island

smoke
storm clouds
volcano
sails
ship
goats
platform
net
driftwood
swamp
spade
rope
shelter
wild pigs
palm trees
rope
ladder
cookin pot
cook
ca
fire
tree
trunk
knife
bottles

The characters

Next, think about the characters.
How do your main characters feel?
Use <u>adjectives</u> (describing words)
to help you. The more interesting
you make the characters, the
more exciting your story will be.

Is this character
a hero, heroine
or a villain?

lightning
sky
lookout
cliff top
cliff
ocean
barrels
sea
waves
sacks
rowing boat
flag
oar
mast
ore
planks
raft
coconuts
cave
apple
bananas
asket
hammocks
rocks

The problem

Adventure stories are action packed! You are the writer and anything can happen.

Perhaps you are attacked...

or disaster strikes...

or something completely unexpected happens.

The setting

Each story is set in a different place. Use your senses to help you describe each place. Think about what you might see, hear, smell, touch and taste.

grassy
leafy

rocky
stony

The resolution

Finally, decide how to end the adventure. What happens? Readers like to know what happens to all the characters. You can choose a happy, sad or surprising ending.

Desert Island

smoke

storm clouds

volcano

sails

ship

goats

platform

net

driftwood

swamp

spade

rope

shelter

tree trunk

wild pigs

palm trees

rope ladder

cook

cooking pot

camp fire

knife

bottles

6

sky

lookout

lightning

cliff top

cliff

horizon

barrels

sea

waves

sacks

rowing
boat

flag

oar

mast

shore

planks

raft

coconuts

cave

pineapple

bananas

basket

hammocks

rocks

sand

7

THE STORY BEGINS

You are on a desert island.
There are many dangers.
You are the hero or heroine.
You have to decide how
to save everyone's life.

Why are you there?
★ Is it your home?
★ Are you shipwrecked?
★ Are you looking for something?

THE CHARACTERS

★ Who lives with you on the island?

friends

shipmates

your family

holiday makers

★ What do you do each day?

gather firewood

catch fish

cook

go swimming

THE SETTING

★ Describe the island.

dry
sandy

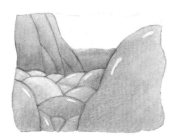
rocky
stony

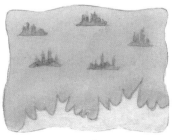
marshy
swampy

grassy
leafy

8

THE PROBLEM

★ Danger ahead! What is it?

creak

splash

A strange ship is approaching.

roar

bellow

snort

rustle

A wild beast attacks.

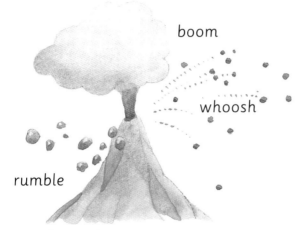

boom

whoosh

rumble

The volcano erupts.

flash

crash

A storm breaks.

Use phrases like these:
To my horror...
I looked up and suddenly saw...
All at once there was a loud...
Out of the blue...

How do you feel?
What do you see?
What do you hear?

THE RESOLUTION

★ What happens in the end?

Do you:
★ hide, and if so, where?
★ lead everyone to safety?
★ sail away on your raft?
★ fight the strangers?

9

Aliens are Here

skyscraper

UFO

fountain

grass

alien

crew

light

satellite dish

fin

aerial

TV light

TV camera

microphone

reporter

van

mobile phone

laptop

crowd

10

helicopter

gates

park

path

banner

band

computer

flag

antennae

leader

platform

chauffeur

president

bodyguard

ramp

steps

steam

robot

video camera

megaphone

limousine

11

THE STORY BEGINS

A UFO has landed in the city centre. Crowds gather in the park to see this astonishing sight. The president hopes the aliens are friendly and has arranged a splendid welcome party.

Decide why the aliens have landed.
★ Has their planet been destroyed?
★ Do they want to conquer earth?
★ Is there something on earth that they desperately need?

THE CHARACTERS

★ Describe the people in your story.

The president could be:

powerful
worried
welcoming
anxious
friendly

The children could be:

inventive
brave
foolish
curious
fearless

The alien leader could be:

threatenir
hopeful
cunning
menacing
grateful

How does he communicate?

THE SETTING

★ Describe the UFO.

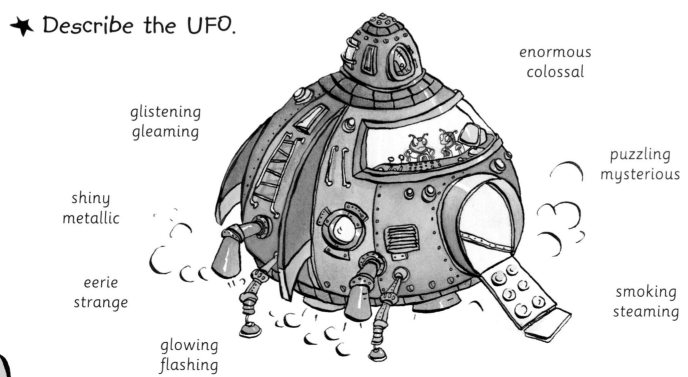

glistening
gleaming

shiny
metallic

eerie
strange

glowing
flashing

enormous
colossal

puzzling
mysterious

smoking
steaming

THE PROBLEM

★ Suddenly the unexpected happens.

Do the aliens attack?

★ What sounds can you hear?

click 'hiss' roar
oompah oompah
chuggah chuggah murmur
nee-naw nee-naw

Does the UFO take off,
leaving the leader behind?

Are the children
kidnapped by the aliens?

Does the President transform
himself into an alien?

Does the alien leader grab
the thing he needs? What is it?

THE RESOLUTION

★ How does the story end?

Remember to tell
your readers what
happens to all
the characters.

★ Do the two leaders make
a deal?

★ Is there a battle?

★ What do the children do?

★ Do the aliens leave or stay?

Princess in Peril

castle

princess

battlements

window

keep

pigs

meadow

steps

king

horses

wood

queen

guard

cauldron

spit

dog

fire

anvil

blacksmith

soldier

wall

sheep

moat

14

banner

hill

turret

cottage

forest

field

village

gatehouse

sword

prince

armour

wagon

drawbridge

horse

path

15

THE STORY BEGINS

A princess is locked in a
tower guarded by two soldiers.
Has she been kidnapped?
Has she done something
terrible and been imprisoned?
Or is she waiting to be rescued?

Here are some ways to begin.

★ No one will find me in the tower...

★ 'She'll never escape,' chuckled
the King.

★ 'How dare they attack me!'
thundered the princess.

THE CHARACTERS

★ Think about the main characters.

Is the princess kind and beautiful?
She could be:

Is the prince brave and handsome?
He could be:

vain
spoilt

superhuman
bloodthirsty

big-headed
greedy

cowardly
clumsy

THE SETTING

★ Where is the castle?

on a hill

beyond the forest

near a village

Is the castle well-kept or is it shabby and dirty?

THE PROBLEM

★ Explain what happens to the princess.

Does she manage to escape? How?

Does she want to be rescued?

Does someone save her life?

Do kidnappers exchange her
for riches, power or land?

★ Add excitement to your story with phrases such as:

Without warning...
Bursting through the door...

Out of the darkness leapt...
In a flash...

THE RESOLUTION

★ What happens in the end?

Write an unexpected
ending to surprise
your readers.

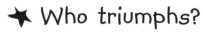

★ Who triumphs?
★ What do they gain?
★ Do the princess and the
prince live happily ever after?

Neptune's Kingdom

air bubbles

oxygen tank

flippers

wet suit

diver

wreck

mast

electric eel

jellyfish

cave

octopus

wheel

tentacles

sand

rope

chain

anchor

camera

coral

spade

angel fish

lobster

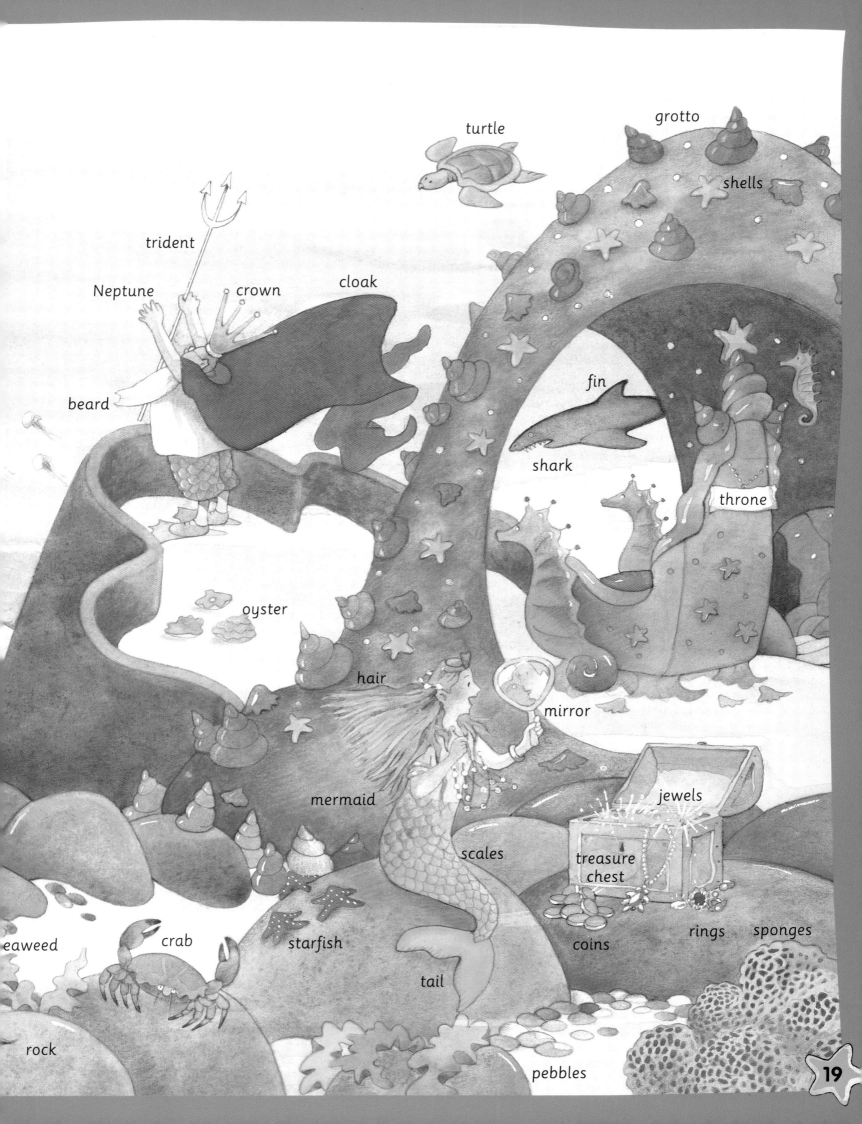

turtle

grotto

shells

trident

Neptune

crown

cloak

fin

beard

shark

throne

oyster

hair

mirror

mermaid

jewels

scales

treasure chest

starfish

rings

sponges

eaweed

crab

coins

tail

rock

pebbles

19

THE STORY BEGINS

Divers have discovered
Neptune's kingdom.
Neptune is an old man,
but he has magic powers.
His kingdom is full
of priceless treasure.

Why have the divers come?
* ★ Are they looking for something?
* ★ Has Neptune asked them
  to come?
* ★ Are they lost?

THE CHARACTERS

★ Decide who to be – a diver, a mermaid or Neptune.

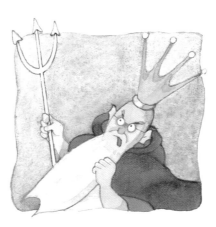

The divers could be:

daring	greedy
curious	adventurous
terrified	bewitched

The mermaid could be:

grateful	annoyed
glad	startled
fearful	excited

Neptune could be:

angry	worried
alarmed	horrified
surprised	amazed

THE SETTING

★ Describe the things you can see.

soggy
spongy

smooth
round

shiny
sparkling

wriggling
gliding

THE PROBLEM

★ What happens when Neptune and the mermaid meet the divers?

Does Neptune:

- assemble a fishy army?
- trick the divers?
- help them?

★ What can you hear?

Does the mermaid:

- fight in the fishy army?
- fall in love with a diver?
- give away her jewels?

Do the divers:

- steal the treasure?
- make friends?
- fight Neptune?

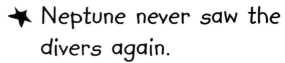

THE RESOLUTION

★ How does your story end?

Here are some ideas for the last line. How could you lead up to this ending?

★ Neptune never saw the divers again.
★ The divers never told anyone about Neptune's Kingdom.
★ The mermaid missed her jewels, but she was proud of saving Neptune.

Rainforest Race

fruit

parrot

jaguar

butterfly

tree

trunk

fungi

creeper

snake

flowers

tree frog

root

mosquitoes

spider

undergrowth

leaves

canopy

monkey

boa
constrictor

oculars

tent

hammock

fern

map

backpack

visor

alligator

compass

tracks

boots

sketch
book

flask

paddle

boulder

torch

sleeping
bag

fishing rod

canoe

ants

23

THE STORY BEGINS

Hidden in the middle of a hot, sticky rainforest is something very precious. You set off to look for it, but discover that other people are looking for it too.

What are you looking for?

★ A rare flower that cures diseases?

★ A lost city?

★ A missing person?

★ Treasure?

THE CHARACTERS

★ Decide which character to be.

Choose words to describe yourself and the other characters.

determined
unselfish
ruthless
greedy
tough
thoughtless
adventurous

THE SETTING

★ What is the rainforest like?

shady
shadowy

hot
damp

steamy
misty

brilliant
colourful

THE PROBLEM

★ On your search you might come across...

a broken bridge

a raging torrent

★ What can you hear?
chattering
rustling
howling
hissing
squawking
screeching

a swarm of insects

ferocious animals

★ These could be clues that you are nearly there.

footprints

smoke from a fire

a funny smell

a sign on a tree

★ Remember your rivals. Can you stop them getting there first?

THE RESOLUTION

★ What happens in the end?

Did you find what you were looking for or have the others beaten you to it?

★ Do you become famous?
★ Will you share your discovery?
★ Can you do a deal?
★ Are you overjoyed or disappointed?

The Marvellous Machine

spanners   hammer   drill   saw   mallet   pliers   file

clock

lamp

torch

screwdrivers

screws

nails

paints
paintbrushes

vice

plans

oil can

robot

cloth

toolbox

spring

steps

mop

bucket

tins

trolley

THE STORY BEGINS

A magnificent machine is hidden in a secret factory. It is the only one in the world. A spy has crept in to find out all about it.

What is special about the machine?
★ What does it make?
★ How does it work?
★ Why is it so secret?

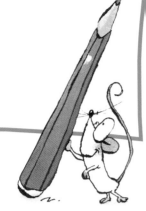

THE CHARACTERS

★ Describe the characters.

One of them could be the spy! Are they:

happy and cheerful
or
cunning and sly

hard-working and clever
or
wicked and scheming

helpful and friendly
or
secretive and sneaky

hot and tired
or
nervous and worried

THE SETTING

★ What is the machine room like?

steamy
smoky

noisy
deafening

messy
untidy

tidy
organized

THE PROBLEM

★ What goes wrong?

Has the machine been reprogrammed?

Has someone spotted the spy?

Does the machine behave oddly?

★ What can you hear?

chug
clatter
CLICK
tick
hum...
rattle
splutter
whirr
CLUNK

Does the spy...

★ escape with the plans?
★ fall into a trap?
★ wreck the machine?

Do the robots stop work?

Has something broken?

THE RESOLUTION

★ What happens in the end?
Your story can end with success for the spy or for the workers.

★ What becomes of the machine?
★ Does the factory stay a secret?
★ What happens to all the characters?

29

WRITING TIPS

Here are some useful tips
to help you start writing
brilliant adventure stories.

What do I need?

First you need to find
a quiet place to write.
You can write with
a pencil on paper or
straight on to a computer. Once you
have written your story you
may want to add some
illustrations.

How do I choose a title?

You could use the story headings in this
book, or you could invent your own title.
Try to make the title sound
exciting so that
everyone will want
to read your story.
Sometimes it is
easier to think
of a title after
writing the story.

How do I start my story?

If you write a gripping opening
everyone will want to read the story.
Here are some ideas.

• Start with one word and
an exclamation mark –
Stop! Run! Help! NO! Quick! Crash!

• Start with a question –
'Where are you going?' asked Sally.

• Start with the name of your main
character – Jim stared out to sea.

How do I make my characters sound real?

Invent two or three main characters and decide what they are like.  Use adjectives to describe them. What sort of people are they – nervous or brave, serious or funny? Are they heroes or villains? How do they speak and what do they say? Make sure they stay the same all through the story!

How do I work out what happens?

Decide how the problem is solved – does the hero or heroine save the day, or does the villain win? Work out what the ending will be before starting to write, and don't forget to say what happens to all the characters. Finish with a really good last line. See if you can think of something more exciting than 'They all lived happily ever after.'

What should I write about?

You need to think of a problem for your characters to face. Maybe they are in danger. What if  a wild animal escaped from a zoo? What if someone cast a wicked spell? You can use the ideas in this book or create your own. Remember to use lots of description.